To Amma, who raised strong Muslim women;
Bahn, my first role model; and my daughters, Rania and Nura.
May Rania stand on our shoulders to reach the stars
where Nura is nestled.
—S. M.


To Dadamma, my very first teacher, who set me on this path
—A. J.

SALAAM
READS

An imprint of Simon & Schuster Children's Publishing Division
1230 Avenue of the Americas, New York, New York 10020
Text copyright © 2019 by Saira Mir
Illustrations copyright © 2019 by Aaliya Jaleel
All rights reserved, including the right of reproduction in whole or in part in any form.
SALAAM READS is a trademark of Simon & Schuster, Inc.
For information about special discounts for bulk purchases, please contact Simon & Schuster Special Sales at
1-866-506-1949 or business@simonandschuster.com.
The Simon & Schuster Speakers Bureau can bring authors to your live event. For more information or to book an event, contact the
Simon & Schuster Speakers Bureau at 1-866-248-3049 or visit our website at www.simonspeakers.com.
Book design by Krista Vossen
The text for this book was set in Radikal.
The illustrations for this book were rendered digitally.
Manufactured in China
0819 SCP
First Edition
2 4 6 8 10 9 7 5 3 1
Names: Mir, Saira, author.
Title: Muslim girls rise : inspirational champions of our time / Saira Mir.
Description: First edition. | New York : Salaam Reads, an imprint of Simon & Schuster Children's Publishing Division, 2019.
Identifiers: LCCN 2018045301 (print) | LCCN 2018046059 (eBook) | ISBN 9781534418882 (hardcover) | ISBN 9781534418899 (eBook)
Subjects: LCSH: Muslim girls—Biography—Juvenile literature. | Muslim women—Biography—Juvenile literature.
Classification: LCC HQ1170 (eBook) | LCC HQ1170 .M566 2019 (print) | DDC 305.23083/297—dc23
LC record available at https://lccn.loc.gov/2018045301

# Muslim Girls Rise

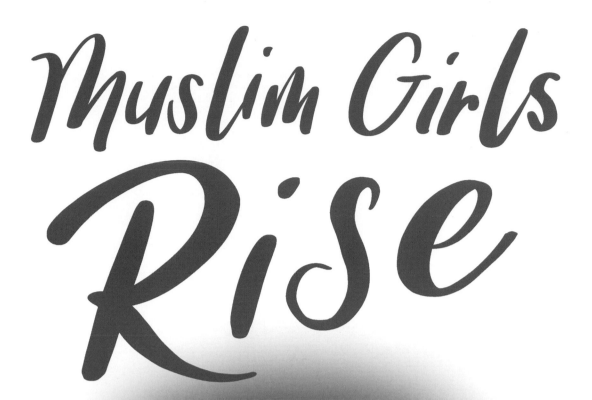

### Inspirational Champions of Our Time

## Saira Mir   *Illustrated by* Aaliya Jaleel

SALAAM
READS

New York  London  Toronto  Sydney  New Delhi

# Rise

verb / ˈrīz

1. to appear above the horizon
2. to increase in intensity
3. to attain a higher level
4. to come into being
5. to exert oneself to meet a challenge

People may tell you that you can't do something because of the way you look, dress, or pray. Your name may sound different. Never forget that you are extraordinary. You are powerful, brave, and clever. Great things come from people like you.

Long ago, Muslim women rode into battle to defend their dreams. They opened the doors to the world's oldest library. They ruled their people, started movements, and spread knowledge.

Today, Muslim women continue to make history.

Once upon a time, they were children with dreams, just like you.

"If there is one thing I have learned, it is that food truly does bring people together."
—Amanda Saab

**Amanda** loved cooking as a child. Growing up in Michigan, she used a stool to reach the counter and help prepare family meals. She discovered the delight of olive oil, garlic, and lemon. Amanda's creativity in the kitchen grew as she did. When she saw an advertisement for a cooking competition on television, she couldn't resist. Amanda whipped up dishes full of flavors from her childhood and became a fan favorite. Although she didn't win the competition, Amanda won the hearts of viewers. She continued using her passion to reach another audience: her neighbors. She opened her home for meals, which she called Dinner with Your Muslim Neighbor. Guests sit at Amanda's table, share delicious food, and ask questions about her life. She hopes to fill the stomachs and hearts of all who dine with her. Amanda believes food can be a path to peace.

**"Never forget that we are strong, and we fight to have our voices rise."**
**—Amani Al-Khatahtbeh**

🔍 muslimgirl.com/    Search

**Amani** **was nine years old when she began hearing negative things about Islam on TV.** Many Americans were scared and suspicious of Muslims. She felt confused and alone. She wanted to speak up and reach out to other girls who felt like her. In her New Jersey high school, she decided to use technology to connect with others, and created a website called MuslimGirl. The site is a platform for Muslim girls to tell the world how they feel about everything from faith to fashion and politics. Millions of people visit her site to read the powerful stories and opinions showcased. Amani has made such an impact, she's been asked to speak with audiences across the country. She has shared stages with world leaders—like former president Bill Clinton—and refuses to be anyone but her real self. Amani wants every Muslim girl to tell her own story.

"It's not in how much or how little you are wearing, but in having choice and the freedom to enact it."
—Hana Tajima

**Hana**'s childhood in England was full of creativity. Her father, a Japanese painter, and mother, a British artist, fueled Hana's imagination. She loved sketching, sewing, and creating clothes for her little sister. It was no surprise that she went on to attend fashion school. Soon after, she started her own design company, Maysaa. Hana's flowing, elegant, and gorgeous clothing gained attention around the world. She caught the eye of the popular company UNIQLO, which asked her to create a womenswear line that included hijabs. Her designs were a hit. Her clothing attracted Muslim customers, but her focus was to create pieces that would make all women feel beautiful. Hana sees fashion as a way of letting your inner artist shine on the outside.

> "Be bold, be fearless, and be confident,
> because you matter."
> —Dalia Mogahed

**Dalia** wanted to make her parents proud, but also follow her heart. After moving to America from her birth country, Egypt, she dreamed of changing the world. She studied science at the University of Wisconsin and became a researcher. She led worldwide studies on Muslim attitudes. She did such a great job, she became an expert on Muslim communities. Dalia was invited to join President Barack Obama's team as an advisor, and was the first Muslim in hijab to advise a U.S. president. She continues to study issues that affect American Muslims, and shares her knowledge so that facts can replace fear. Dalia knows that listening to your heart is how you make real change.

"The experiences of my life have taught me to always dream big and to never give up."
—Hibah Rahmani

**Hibah** was fascinated by the magic of the night sky. During evening walks with her family, she would look up at the stars and wonder about astronauts who had walked on the moon. She loved science and math so much that at the age of eight she wanted to be an engineer. Nothing would stop her. When war broke out in her country, Kuwait, Hibah escaped to safety in the middle of the night. She slept under the open sky in the cold desert. In that moment, she looked up to see a beautiful view of the stars and was reminded of her dream. Today Hibah launches spaceships as a flight control engineer at NASA. She hopes to one day become an astronaut. Hibah literally reaches for the stars.

**Ibtihaj** **loved playing sports.** She enjoyed everything from tennis to softball and volleyball. Sometimes she felt like she stuck out from the other athletes in her hometown of Maplewood, New Jersey, because she covered her arms, legs, and hair. She never let that feeling hold her back, though, and continued doing what she loved. One day she saw kids practicing fencing, a sword-fighting sport. She noticed the uniform they wore was hijab-friendly. When she tried fencing, the strong, fast pace of the saber was a perfect fit. With years of hard work, she won many championships and a prized spot on the U.S. Olympic fencing team. Ibtihaj was the first Muslim in hijab to represent the United States. She made history again by bringing home a medal. Ibtihaj encourages girls to feel confident and strong through sports.

**"Do not let others place limitations on your abilities; be limitless."**
**—Ilhan Omar**

**Ilhan** **fled war in Somalia at age eight.** She spent many years living in refugee camps before her family found a new home in the United States. Her grandfather attended local political meetings and asked her to join. At these meetings, Ilhan was inspired by neighbors joining hands to make a difference. She found ways to get involved in her community as well. Ilhan became a policy analyst, someone who helps solve problems in their community. Her passion for serving others led her all the way to one of the highest offices in the state of Minnesota. She made history as the first Somali-American elected to the Minnesota House of Representatives. Ilhan fights for important issues like fairness and gender equality. In 2019, she began serving as the U.S. Representative for Minnesota's 5th congressional district.

"My greatest accomplishment is the ability to love.
It's easy for me to do the work that I do,
because I love unconditionally."
—Ilyasah Shabazz

**Ilyasah** lost her father when she was only two years old. Her father was Malcolm X, a famous civil rights leader who fought for equality. Equality means all people should be treated fairly. Ilyasah heard incredible stories about the man she barely knew. She carried on her father's dream and wrote award-winning books about his life. She motivates kids to get educated, get along with others, and love themselves. Ilyasah has traveled the world to meet with leaders and celebrate peace. She helps encourage people from different religions to work together. Ilyasah believes that focusing on love can erase hate.

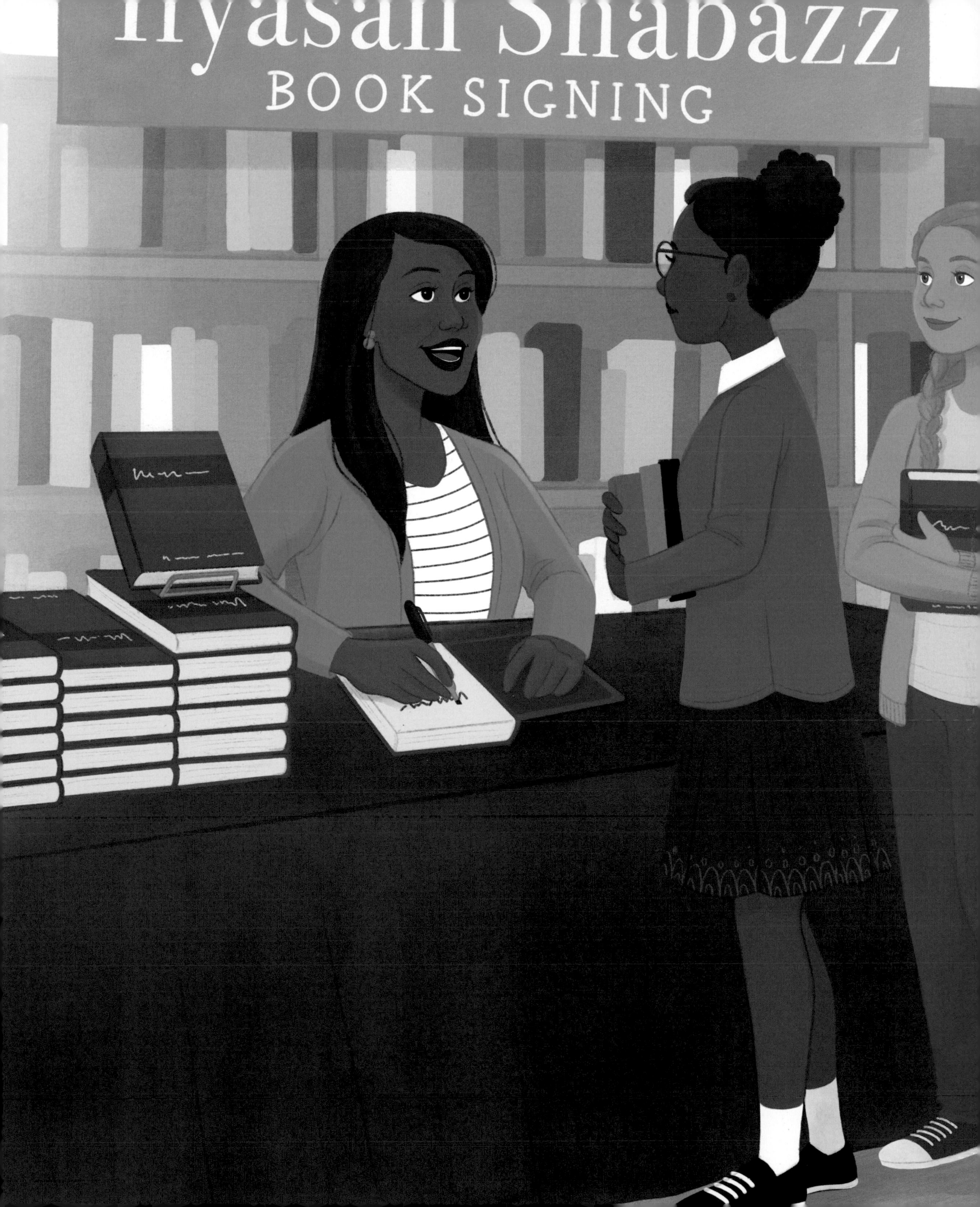
Ilyasah Shabazz
BOOK SIGNING

This is what a **FEMINIST** looks like

STRONG WOMEN
KNOW THEM. BE THEM. RAISE THEM.

"Generations from now, little girls and boys will hold their chests out with pride, reading about the leadership of women who united a divided nation."
—Linda Sarsour

WOMEN'S RIGHTS = HUMAN RIGHTS

**Linda** **feels happiest when she's standing up to bullies and defending others.** She is an activist. Schools in New York recognize Eid as a holiday because of her efforts. President Barack Obama honored her with the Champion of Change award for her extraordinary efforts in the community. In 2017, she led the largest protest for human rights in American history, called the Women's March on Washington. When Linda sees someone's actions hurting others, she speaks up and works toward change.

> "One child, one teacher, one book, and one pen can change the world."
> —Malala Yousafzai

# Malala wanted one thing growing up: to learn.

As the daughter of a teacher, she knew knowledge is power. In the beautiful landscape of Swat Valley, Pakistan, where Malala grew up, weak men tried to force girls to stay at home. They wanted to keep women powerless. When she continued to go to school and spoke against inequality, she was attacked. Malala survived a violent attempt to end her life, and her voice only grew stronger. She fights for every girl's right to attend school all over the world. Because of her efforts, she was the youngest person, at age seventeen, to win the Nobel Peace Prize. Malala wants all girls to have the power of an education.

"I want to tell girls fear is taught; you were born free and you were born brave."
—Maria Toorpakai Wazir

**Maria** grew up in an area of Pakistan where men told women what they could and could not do. At age four, she refused to be controlled. She burned her dresses, cut her hair, and lived her childhood as a boy. Her father even started calling her "Genghis Khan" after one of the most feared warriors in history. Maria stood her ground and sometimes got into fights with boys. Her father wanted to channel her energy into something positive, so he introduced her to the sport of squash. Maria loved the high-energy game. She did well and quickly rose to the top in her country. When Maria finally revealed she was a girl, men bullied her. Maria was courageous. She did not give up playing and found a trainer to help her become a world champion. Maria believes that no one should ever stand between a girl and her dreams.

**"I don't give up easily."
—Maryam Mirzakhani**

**Maryam** relished stories of young heroines. She dreamed of becoming a writer. With the guidance of a supportive teacher, she discovered exciting stories with different characters: numbers. Mathematics was a world of mystery and adventure. With her newfound passion, Maryam represented Iran in an international mathematics competition. She won gold in her first match and sealed a perfect score in the next. She went on to study and then teach math in the U.S. She drew her ideas on paper, flowery figures and loopy rings, all part of an equation she was trying to solve. Her work was groundbreaking, making her the first woman to earn a Fields Award, the highest honor in math. Until her death in 2017, Maryam used her knowledge to unlock mathematical mysteries that explain how the world works.

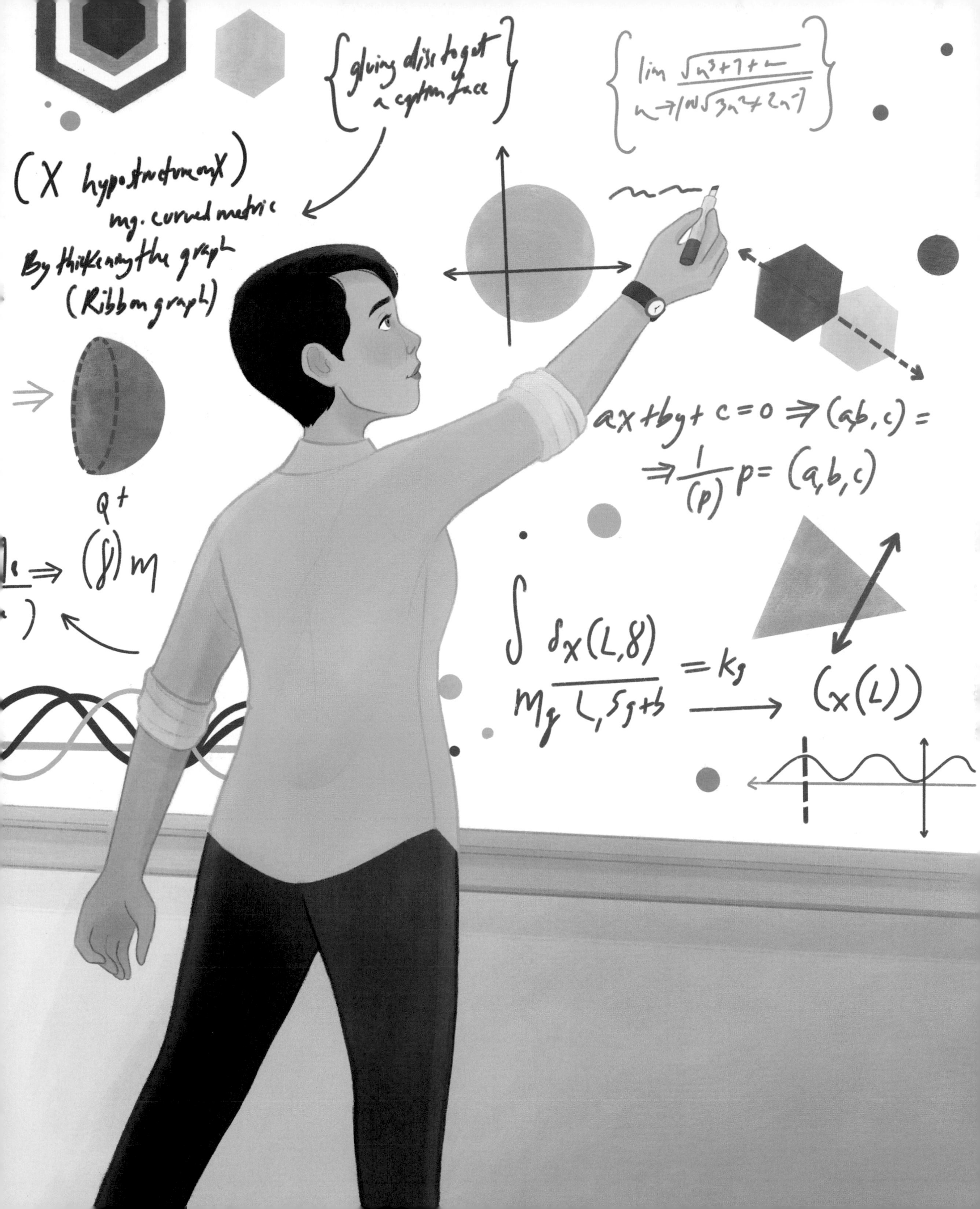

(Ribbon graph)
ax+by+c=0 ⇒ (a,b,c) =

"For me, a refugee name gives me strength to create a bright future from my hard situation. We are not just refugees, we are not just children—we can make a change."
—Muzoon Almellehan, *Teen Vogue*

**Muzoon** escaped the war in Syria at age fourteen. She traveled through several countries and refugee camps. Life as a refugee was hard for many reasons, but her greatest concern was missing school. Her father, a teacher, had instilled in her a love of learning. It's hard to focus on long-term goals when food, safety, and shelter are concerns, but she didn't want refugees to lose hope. In the camps, she urged parents to send their daughters to school because she knew education is the key to a brighter future. Global leaders listened when she carried her message to the United Nations. Muzoon wants all children to have the right to an education.

> "When you approach people with love,
> you get love in return."
> —Negin Farsad

*Negin* felt like an outsider growing up in New Haven, Connecticut, until she discovered the magical world of drama club in high school. She met other kids like her: creative, original, and quirky. Being on stage and making others laugh felt good. Later, she realized that as a Muslim woman in comedy, she had a unique voice. Her voice needed to be heard. Negin gathered a group of American Muslim comedians and hit the road. Her show was called *The Muslims Are Coming!* This tour helped people across America meet Muslims who made them laugh and opened their minds. Negin knows the power of a smile to connect strangers.

> **"Just because you don't look like everyone else doesn't mean you're any less than anyone else."**
> **—Nura Afia**

**Nura liked to play with makeup.** As a teenager in Aurora, Colorado, she rimmed her eyes with kohl. Over time she began experimenting with different styles of makeup. Carefully blending shimmering shadows across her eyelids or sweeping rich stain across her lips, her face became a canvas to express herself. Nura wanted to share her love of makeup with others. She began creating online videos, which drew a lot of attention. CoverGirl cosmetics asked her to join them in a beauty campaign. Nura stood alongside people of different races and genders to shoot a commercial on beauty equality. Her smiling face was spread across a billboard in Times Square. By being herself, Nura helped change the face of beauty in America.

"**Good is not a thing you are.
It's a thing you do.**"
**—Ms. Marvel, created by
Sana Amanat and G. Willow Wilson**

# Kamala Khan, also known as Ms. Marvel,

is an average Pakistani-American teenager who discovers she has shape-shifting powers.

She is the brainchild of two Muslim women: Sana Amanat and G. Willow Wilson. Both Sana and Willow know the power of stories to make kids feel inspired and empowered—they experienced it in their own childhoods, gravitating to comic books that featured characters whose differences were their strengths. No longer a kid, Sana is vice president of content and character development at Marvel Comics, where she teamed up with fellow comic book lover G. Willow Wilson to create Kamala.

Kamala struggles with figuring out life, while balancing her parents' expectations and saving her hometown from evil geniuses. Not easy, but Kamala rises to the occasion. Ms. Marvel shows all readers that being a hero is about being you.

"Never take no for an answer. If a door hasn't opened up for you, it's because you haven't kicked it hard enough."
—Sharmeen Obaid-Chinoy

**Sharmeen** always enjoyed storytelling. At age seventeen she was a writer for a Pakistani national newspaper and went undercover to investigate bullying. The day her story was published, someone spray-painted threats outside her home. Her father turned to Sharmeen and said, "If you speak the truth, I will stand with you and so will the world." Sharmeen never looked back. She continued seeking out stories and eventually turned to film-making. Today she makes films about brave women who suffer unfair treatment. Her work has earned her international recognition and awards, including Academy Awards and Emmy awards. Audiences learn about changes needed to make our world a better place. Her films have also helped inspire laws to protect women from violence and injustice. Sharmeen wants to make the world a fairer place, one story at a time.

"It's not just about hope and ideas. It's about action. . . ."
—Shirin Ebadi

**Shirin** was the daughter of a teacher in Iran. She had a passion for learning and did well in school. Through her studies she gained a degree in law and became the country's first female judge. Shortly after, Iran fell into the hands of men who wanted control in the name of religion. They took away her right to be a judge. She spent many frustrating years unable to work. When she was finally allowed to become a lawyer, she fought to protect women, children, and political prisoners in Iran. She herself was threatened, bullied, and jailed by the government. Shirin became the first Muslim woman to win a Nobel Peace Prize. Although her prize was stolen by the government and she was forced to leave the country, she has remained outspoken. Shirin knows the right to live free is worth fighting for.

**Muslim women make history every day.** Some have risked their lives defending their beliefs. Others had to leave their homes for freedom. All of these women followed their heart. By refusing to give up, they achieved greatness.

# Find your passion, and like these women, you will RISE.

Connect like Amanda.

Empower like Amani.

Create like Hana.

Teach like Dalia.

Reach like Hibah.

Focus like Ibtihaj.

Lead like Ilhan.

Love like Ilyasah.

March like Linda.

Defy like Malala.

Persist like Maria.

Solve like Maryam.

Advocate like Muzoon.

Redefine like Nura.

Laugh like Negin.

Represent like Sana.

Envision like Willow.

Uncover like Sharmeen.

Defend like Shirin.

# Bibliography

Al-Khatahtbeh, Amani. "A Letter to My Future Muslim Daughter."
    *Cosmopolitan*, October 9, 2017. https://www.cosmopolitan.com/
    politics/a7557079
    /amani-al-khatahtbeh-muslim-girl-daughter-letter/.

Dwyer, Kate. "Meet an 18-Year-Old Syrian Refugee Who Is
    Championing Girls' Education Rights." *Teen Vogue*, May 25, 2017.
    https://www.teenvogue.com/story/syrian-refugee-muzoon
    -almellehan-championing-girls-education-rights.

Granath, Bob. "Hard Work, Focus, Helps Rahmani Reach for the
    Stars." NASA. April 2, 2014. https://www.nasa.gov/content
    /hard-work-focus-helps-rahmani-reach-for-the-stars.

Heidenreich, Erin, dir. *Girl Unbound: The War to Be Her*. 2016.
    Blackacre Entertainment. https://thewartobeher.com/band/.

Kantor, Jessica. "Muslim Beauty Vlogger Nura Afia on Confidence,
    Breastfeeding, and Her Impressive Two-Hour Makeup Routine."
    *Glamour*, March 9, 2017. https://www.glamour.com/story
    /nura-afia-beauty.

Karins, Jessica. "Ilyasah Shabazz Reflects on Father Malcolm X's
    Legacy." *The Journal*, April 5, 2016.
    http://websterjournal.com/2016/04/05
    /ilyasah-shabazz-reflects-on-father-malcolm-xs-legacy/.

Klarreich, Erica. "Meet the First Woman to Win Math's Most
    Prestigious Prize." *Wired*, August 13, 2014. https://www.wired
    .com/2014/08/maryam-mirzakhani-fields-medal/.

Muhammad, Ibtihaj. "Ibtihaj Muhammad: I Fear President Trump's
    'Campaign of Terror' Against American Ideals." Time.com, March
    20, 2017. time.com/4706627
    /olympic-fencer-ibtihaj-muhammad-donald-trump/.

Permanent Secretariat of the World Summit of Nobel Peace
    Laureates. "Meet the Laureates: Shirin Ebadi, Nobel Peace Prize
    2003." World Summit of Nobel Peace Laureates. www.nobel-
    peacesummit.com
    /meet-the-laureates-shirin-ebadi-nobel-peace-prize-2003/.

Saab, Amanda. "About." Amanda's Plate. 2018. http://
    amandasplate.com/about/.

Sarsour, Linda. "#WhyIMarch." Women's Media Center. January 13,
    2017. http://www.womensmediacenter.com/news-features
    /whyimarch.

Stansfield, Ted. "The Designer behind Uniqlo's First UK Hijab Range."
    *Dazed*. March 21, 2016. http://www.dazeddigital.com/fashion
    /article/30450/1
    /meet-the-designer-behind-uniqlo-s-first-uk-hijab-range.

Williams, Mary Elizabeth. "WATCH: Negin Farsad on Being a Pop Tart-
    Loving Muslim American and Breaking the Muslim Stereotype."
    Salon, January 17, 2017. https://www.salon.com/2017/01/18
    /watch-negin-farsad-on-being-a-pop-tart-
    loving-muslim-american-and-breaking-the-muslim-stereotype/.

Wilson, G. Willow. *Ms. Marvel Volume 5: Super Famous*. New York:
    Marvel, 2016.

Yousafzai, Malala, with Patricia McCormick. *I Am Malala: How One
    Girl Stood up for Education and Changed the World*. Boston, MA:
    Little, Brown Books for Young Readers, 2015.